Autism Inspires!

Hope as a Parent's Savior

by Lena McCalla Njee

minna
PRESS
www.minnapress.com

ISBN: 978-0-9829630-8-1

Revised Edition

www.lenamccallabooks.com

Illustrations by Elizabeth Gauthier

Published by Minna Press

Kingston • New York • Charlotte

“Lena McCalla Njee’s work has transformed the lives of many individuals. Her sensitive and insightful look into the challenges that children with autism face is written eloquently and with compassion.”

Nazin Abdul-Rahim MS CCC-SLP

Table of Contents

FOREWORD

It was indeed a great pleasure to write the foreword to this book, *Autism Inspires!* With the drastic increase in autism, especially with boys (1 in 100 boys born each day), I am delighted that the author has written this book. It is a thoughtful blend of optimism and hope.

Isn't this what we want most?

This book should be given to all parents in schools with autism-diagnosed children, as this will allow parents to be more optimistic about their child's ability to learn and improve. Autism can affect your family, friends or neighbors. This easy to read book can also provide more awareness to others.

Getting an autism diagnosis for my son Kye at the age of two left our family feeling hopeless. We had to quickly adjust to living in a bubble, as some folks would become uncomfortable having Kye's unusual behaviors at their functions. Frankly, we got tired of chasing Kye around to ensure he did not touch people's TV when he became fascinated by the colors. We became tired of taking him off people's couches because he was feeling over-stimulated and needed to jump. We had to get used to not being invited to many places.

We thought that having Kye in a Montessori school would at least allow him to be creative, but we were asked to remove him from the school because his behavior was a little out of the teacher's comfort zone. Enrolling Kye into Ms. Lena's class was one of the best things we've done for Kye and our family.

The first day we met Ms. Lena, she greeted us with such optimism, she stressed the importance of accepting and praising Kye's every accomplishment, even if seemed insignificant. I agreed to try these suggestions and I began to accept Kye for who he was. Ms. Lena suggested taking him out on trips, and that's what we did. We travelled locally and internationally; we took him to the restaurants and the mall. Yes, we sometimes had challenging moments, but we never gave up. Instead, I sometimes explained to folks that Kye has autism, so if he cut into a line, it was because he is still learning the concept of waiting. Many people understand, and that fills our journey with hope for understanding.

The one thing Ms. Lena told us that left us skeptical was that Kye could learn. I would ask my husband how it was possible to teach a child who bounces around the room. Everyday, Ms. Lena would send home a new praise, but the day she wrote and called in excitement that Kye could use a computer mouse, I told myself I needed to see it to believe. Kye, now being five years old, is great with the computer, and a great speller, thanks to Ms. Lena and staff. Without Ms. Lena's ray of hope, Kye would not be this advanced.

Knowing Ms. Lena was always there to listen and encourage us made our journey with autism full of hope. We are anticipating seeing what Kye will become. Possibly he will be an inventor, and we're excited to share our excitement with him. Each and every day, we let Kye know how great he is as a person; and this was made possible by this author.

The information presented in this book offers quick-needed information for the overall benefit of families dealing with autism. You can expect to find information that will allow families to gain a great sense of hope and optimism. *Autism Inspires!* was written with the intent to give surmountable hope to families.

Expect to benefit greatly from this book. It is filled with real experiences that the number-one teacher in the district for 2011, encounters while working daily with children of autism. This book shows that Lena McCalla believes that every child is a gift that we are given and that each child can learn in his or her own way. Lena's optimism and belief in each of these children proved to be a ray of hope for many families.

This book should also serve as inspiration for many parents as they are able to learn and identify with various stories. From the reading, we'll see that all these children improved in some way, and this certainly allows parents to have hope. Such hope can transform your child and allow him to accomplish anything.

I believe this book will impact the lives of many, as it is an excellent source of information regarding the power of being hopeful.

This engaging, easy to read book reflects the caring optimistic characteristics of Lena McCalla and her quest to inspire children with autism. Ms. Lena should be congratulated for this thoughtful approach, and everyone who is fortunate to read this book will find it instrumental in their child's improvement.

- By Teresitia Walters, MA, MPA, Doctoral Candidate
Student Development Specialist/Founder of Autism Awake
Seton Hall University, South Orange NJ

INTRODUCTION

In my role as the teacher, I do not pretend to walk in these parents' shoes. Neither do I claim to understand their pain. I am with their children for six hours daily, but these parents have to be there for their children twenty-four/seven.

I listen, empathize, support and encourage every one of my parents to be advocates for their children who have special needs. I aspire to be the best teacher to their children. Part of my core philosophy as a teacher is that all children can learn. Children have different styles of learning, different rates of learning, and will acquire different levels of learning.

I treat my children only as 'special' as they need to be treated. I encourage my parents to do the same. Yes! I do see all the children as 'my' children and I try to form a relationship with their parents so we can work as a team to support the children. I tell parents not to lose sight of the hope and dreams for their children just because they have autism or any other disabilities. Because a child has autism, I do not believe that he should not be educated in social competence, self-help skills, language, mathematics, science, social studies and all other aspects of a broad education.

I encourage parents to take their children, despite their disabilities, on vacation, out on trips, just like they would take any of their other children. Take them to the zoo, parks, restaurant, supermarkets, church functions, and family gatherings. Of course as a parent of a child with special needs, parents have to be cognizant that they will have to make some modifications in order for these trips to be successful. I tell parents not to be embarrassed when or if their autistic child acts out in public. How many times have we seen normal children yelling and acting out in the aisle? A child with autism is not so very different. He has to be taught to manage himself in different situations. In fact, parents can use the moment when some stranger stare at their child in awe as a teachable moment to educate someone who has never heard of autism or has never seen a child with autism.

Parents need to be aware of the triggers that will set their child off. They need not avoid those triggers, but slowly expose the child to them and teach the child how to manage himself in unpleasant circumstances. Loud noises, such as those emanated from an ambulance, fire truck and police car can upset the child. That does not mean the child cannot be exposed to such noises.

There are many things that can be done to help a child adjust to such noises: for instance, the parents can introduce the child to a toy fire truck with a siren or a puzzle of a fire truck which will make a sound when the pieces are put in the right slots. Parents can also pass by the fire station and point out a real fire truck. From a distance, acknowledge police cars or the ambulances as you come across them in the daily life of the child.

Eventually, parents can plan a short trip to see a fire truck up close. Most fire chiefs will be delighted to let a child climb up and even sit in the fire truck at the station. Who knows—the child may even be tolerant of the chief pulling the loud horn of the truck while he is sitting in it.

In the ensuing chapters, I will share personal stories about some of the many children that I have taught over the years. Included are coping skills and activities in the stories that all parents can use and share. You can also explore the comprehensive resource materials that will be beneficial in your daily interactions with your child.

My hope is that parents will find humor, comfort and solace in these stories and look beyond the disabilities and see the child for his uniqueness and his abilities. I hope too that this book will promote greater tolerance, acceptance and inclusion for children with autism, and for all children no matter their disability.

- By Lena McCalla Njee
Author and Special Education Teacher

INSPIRATIONAL STORIES OF CHILDREN WITH AUTISM

When I enter the classroom, I am a teacher, but I am also a mother. I tell parents I may not know all the intricacies of their particular situation, but I am a parent too. These short stories that I am about to share are factual except for the fictional names or initials or settings, which are used to safeguard the backgrounds and the children's identities.

Horace

Every day for almost a year, Horace would sit in circle time and rock back and forth. He never uttered a word. Never made a sustained eye contact. Each day I would conduct circle time in the same routine.

I tried to teach the children about the weather, colors, shapes, numbers, self awareness, name identification, how to picture read, listening and such.

One day unexpectedly, Horace jumped up and started counting. He ran up to the number chart and started to point to each of the numbers as he counted. My assistants and I were amazed. One of the children shouted, "He talks, he talks."

We whooped and hollered so loudly that other teachers came out in the hallway to see if they could catch a glimpse of what the commotion was about in my room. The principal came hurriedly to the room. We all were in awe.

Horace could talk.

When I shared the good news with Horace's mother, she cried uncontrollably. After she was able to contain her tears of joy, she tried to apologize. She looked me in the eye and said, "Ms. Lena, you don't know what it feels like to have a five-year-old who never said your name." Now, it was my turn to break down. I found myself hugging Horace's mom and the tears rolled down my face. I looked up and all the other adults in the room were crying. I took the liberty to say to this parent, "Yes, I understand." I believe that until you have walked in someone's shoes, you are never in a position to really understand the depth or the burden of her pain.

It seemed like the floodgate to Horace's vocabulary stream had suddenly opened. His vocabulary kept expanding daily. He hardly ever kept quiet. He graduated from my class at the end of that school year.

Horace eventually acquired skills to function in an inclusion class with peers who were not classified with any special needs. His parents are very hopeful of the future.

Quincy

The first day I met Quincy, he was literally dragged kicking and screaming into my classroom by his grandmother and another family member. Of course I had been told in advance that he was scheduled to visit my class.

Quincy's grandmother was his legal guardian. He was assigned to my class and it took several days of crying for him to begin to settle in.

Quincy's challenging behaviors included spitting, hitting, biting, and throwing food. He had no expression of verbal language. His mode of communication was pointing, pulling and yelling.

As the days turned into weeks and the weeks turned into months, I noticed that Quincy had a fondness for magazines and newspapers. He would turn the pages and look at the pictures as if he were analyzing and making sense of the print and the pictures. I started to bring all types of magazines into the classroom.

One day I noticed that Quincy was looking at the TV Guide section of the newspaper. I said to myself, what on earth could be fascinating from the TV Guide?

I decided to probe further, and then I started utilizing the newspaper and the magazines in teaching fine motor and other skills such as tearing, cutting, painting, left to right sequencing, shape identification and language arts. He was making headway in terms of receptive cognitive skills. His social and self-help skills were at a standstill.

The daily spitting, scratching and resistance to being toilet trained continued. Grandma said she was willing to toilet train him at home, and at school we had him on a schedule. At school he was not allowed to keep pampers on. He had a lot of "potty incidents."

Grandma came in one morning to report that she forgot to tell us that she had stopped trying to get him to use the potty standing up and he was being trained at home sitting down. OK! We switched to having him sit in school so we could maintain the consistency. My thinking was that he could learn to aim at a later date once he started going in the potty. He was terrified of the sound of the water as the toilet flushed. The toilet was set to flush by motion and sometimes it flushed while he sat.

Standing up should have been less challenging, or so I thought. Now Quincy had the bright idea that he could put his foot in the toilet every time. One day both socks and shoes came off in the toilet and I had to reach in to get them out as the toilet flushed. We now had to turn the water off from the tank every time Quincy had to use it. Now the toilet was no longer flushing on its own. Eventually he sat without the constant yelling. He finally started to pee in the potty sitting down. One day he finally pooped in the potty. I felt all the scratches and the battling had been worth the trouble. Certainly it was one of the most beautiful poops ever. I was so excited I called all the adults to take a look. Quincy looked at his production as if he were amazed. He then started to push us away as if to make sure we did not flush it. Potty training from that day was a 'breeze.' We were able to retrain him to stand when he peed and sit when he needed to.

He started to respond to verbal praise and tangible rewards such as Cheerios and stickers. He mastered potty training to the extent where he would sign or just go when he wanted.

One day while I was reading to Quincy, I accidentally skipped one of the pages. He started to cry and flap his arms. I returned to the skipped page and he became quiet and started to smile. I said to myself, "No way."

I wondered if he was really understanding that I had skipped part of the story, so a little further along, I deliberately skipped a page, and sure enough his reactions were the same. He yelled and flapped and threw a tantrum. I was convinced that, if he could not read, he at least understood the sequencing of the story and there was no way of tricking him. This was a child who had previously exhibited no verbal skills.

His strength, I determined, was visual memorization and sequencing. Programs were designed and taught to his strengths. He was assigned a therapist who taught him to sign. Quincy became a joy to work with. By the time he left my class, he had started to sign and use some functional words. He was fully potty trained before he left my class, and he had started to play alongside other children. On few occasions, he had exchanged toys with his peers. Therein for me was more than a ray of hope.

Devon

Devon my darling! Oh how he could break a heart when he occasionally made eye contact with those beautiful eyes. He loved to hum and move rhythmically, I might add. I never got a verbal response from Devon, but on one particular day, I received an earful of surprise from him. It was quiet time and I sat on the carpet beside him. Everyone was asleep or lying quietly on cots. The only obvious disturbance in the air was the quiet constant humming from Devon, who was one of the non-sleepers.

One of the sleeping children passed gas and it did not escape Devon's notice. He exclaimed, "Oh! Oh, he farted." I could not believe what I heard. This child had never talked in my presence. I said, "What?" Sure enough, he repeated his comment. My side was splitting with laughter.

When one of the assistants walked in, she too started to wail with laughter when I told her. That verbal expression from Devon was clear, loud and precise. This boy had the ability to talk; he had selective speech and I was determined to help design a language-rich program that would provoke his expressive skills. The speech therapist and I helped to design activities around rhythm and movements. He was still not using functional words, but he gave echoic responses.

There would be sessions when we would have him listen to and echo the words that were said to him. He then started to identify some pictures when they were visually presented. We no longer accepted a point or a pull from Devon. He was given the words when he pointed and he was forced to use words in lieu of his points and pulls.

It was very important that all members of the team were on board in helping to encourage Devon's language. When he pointed to something, he was given the words and the pictures from the PECS (Picture Exchange Communication System). I am always hopeful and looking for a breakthrough when the child with the ability starts to speak.

Devon loved pretzels, but he had to be watched carefully when he ate them so that he would not consume too much in his mouth. On this particular day, it was snack time and Devon was required to say, "Pretzel, please," along with making the "more" sign for every piece he wished to have.

After complying for a few pieces, Devon decided he was not going to say pretzel please, and he was not going to make the "more sign." Neither would he give the picture for pretzel. Snack time was coming to an end and one of the assistants started to sing the "clean up" song.

Devon stood up and yelled, "Gi mee moore pretzels please." Boy! I was unprepared for all that outburst. He was allowed to have all the pretzels he wanted then. From that day on, I never accepted less than I knew he could give.

It is very important that all the members on the team and in the child's life keep up the momentum in getting the child to practice speaking at every opportunity. If demands are not put on most children with autism to speak, they will continue to point and throw tantrums to get what they want and need. Grandma had started to hear verbal expressions at home as well. She was encouraged to hold out on his "demands" and have him replace his pointing with speaking.

I know it's hard for parents when they have had a hard day at work and then they must come home and insist that a child says "milk" instead of just handing it to him when he points and has a tantrum. However, the more words the child acquires and uses functionally, the more independent he will become and the less behavioral challenges will be presented. It is important for home and school to be on the same page. Hope is a motivator.

I tell my parents to never give up and never give in. I encourage them to take a break, but get right back on track. Challenge your child, embrace his weaknesses. Keep pushing your child to maximize his potential. All children can learn. Your child can learn. Some learn differently. I have never met a child who could not learn and I have never met a child I could not teach. It is our job as parents, teachers, therapists, and all stake holders to teach to the child's strengths and improve his weaknesses.

MISS PRINCESS

I called her Miss Princess because of all the beautiful frilly dresses she often wore when she started attending my class. She looked like a princess.

I had to beg her mother to allow her to wear some sweat suits and play shoes. She needed to make mud pies and finger paint like every other child, without having to worry about her clothes getting ruined. When we met, she was not potty trained. I mostly always bring up potty-training at the first meeting with the parents, because being potty trained helps the child develop self-esteem.

With increased self-esteem and potty-training out of the way, there will be more time to focus on communication, social, self help and other skills. Her parents were all excited about starting potty-training as soon as she started school.

It was evident that her parents were working with her at home, and she was an easy candidate for potty-training. Potty-training was smooth sailing for her.

I don't usually start potty training until the parents are ready. I am not one to try to usurp the parents' authority or try to make it seem I want to take the decision-making away from them.

In essence, the work becomes futile if the child is being potty-trained at school and there is no follow-up at home. I recognize the accomplishment in the eyes when the child is able to indicate that he needs to go and does it. I present reasons why the child needs to learn to use the potty.

Usually if all else fails, the parents will consider it when I show them in dollars and cents. I will say something like, “Mom, if you are spending an average of $30.00 weekly just for Pampers, that will total $120 monthly and will add up to $1,440.00 annually.” Their eyes will light up when they see the economic aspect of potty-training. For some parents, money is not an issue and it is their right to decide when to start potty-training their child.

Ms. Princess had the ability to talk. At first she would speak only French, especially when she got excited. Her parents said they spoke to her at home mostly in English. Once she got a command of the English language, her vocabulary started to expand and some of her negative behaviors decreased.

She had many challenges in social skills. Everything was “mine.” Even when there were more of the same items, she would hoard whatever she fancied at the moment. She would yell and scream when she had to give up anything she wanted to keep.

If allowed, she would eat her food and everyone else’s. It took quite some time for her to learn that it was not okay for her to reach in another child’s plate and take whatever she wanted. Because Miss Princess has autism, that doesn’t mean she is incapable of learning proper table manners.

"Every child can learn." Frequently, I remind my parents never to lose sight of that hope. Parents must have the same high expectation for all their children, whether they are diagnosed with a disability or not.

TRIM & SYKE

Then I met the brothers. I called them Trim and Syke. After meeting and talking to the parents, my heart ached. It was challenging enough to have one child with special needs, but two, I thought, was insurmountable. When the parents told me they had a third child with special needs, I quietly said to myself, I will never complain again about a single thing.

After the observations of my class, the parents made the decision to separate the boys into different classes. I believed that was a good decision to ensure that each would get a chance to develop his own identity away from the other sibling.

The brother in my class was a master spitter. His spitting was greatest when he was frustrated. He would spit so much that sometimes his shirt was soaking wet. The parents had suggested that he should wear a bib. I told them that I was totally against it. I did not want the other kids who could talk to tease him. He did not need to be treated differently. He needed to learn to communicate and to stop this inappropriate behavior. He liked to assemble puzzles. However, if he was having difficulty getting a piece in its right slot, the whole set would be thrown across the room and anyone in his path became a target for his spit missiles.

He had one-on-one assistants for most of his activities. He eventually became adept at assembling all types of puzzles. After Trim was able to use the picture cards combined with some functional signs to communicate, his spitting rampage decreased. He started to have fewer tantrums.

He was paired with an excellent speech therapist, who worked with him extensively one-on-one, as well as in a small group. He had started to use some functional words and phrases. His eye contact was more sustained and his self help skills started to improve. He was washing and drying his own hands and he was frequently demanding what he wanted with signs and words. His self confidence improved right along.

One interesting aspect of the two brothers was the lack of interaction when they met in the gym or in the cafeteria. They were oblivious of each other. One would not think that the brothers knew each other. I never witnessed them looking at or playing with each other.

After a year the family moved out of town. Both parents stopped in to see me before the move and they both expressed gratitude over the growth of both boys. They reported that they had seen improvement in all domains. The parents left with hope and dreams for all three children. Hope has to be a mother's savior when she is blessed with not one, not two, but three children with autism.

TRACK STAR

Here comes…there goes…Track Star. My goodness! Seems like she was always running. We could not let go of her hand when she was out of the classroom. She would run straight for the door. She had knocked over more than a few children in the hallway and in the gym. She had no sense of danger. She ran into people and objects alike.

Once I got to know her mother, I learned that Track Star had run away from her on several occasions. I invited her on several class trips as chaperone, but she explained because of her work schedules, she was never able to attend.

Track Star's mother told me she had not been to church in years and taking her out in public was out of the question. She said her daughter had become a total distraction in the church service. Some members in the church had also made unkind comments about her not being proactive and that she was unable to control her child.

After Track Star was with us for about a year, her mother told me she was going to take her to visit the mall. I told her to be careful and be sure to wear her

running shoes. I said that with tongue-in-cheek. I was hopeful that she would have a good trip with her daughter.

If she had asked my suggestion, perhaps I would have told her to take her to the park a few times before she ventured in the mall. As a teacher, my role is to support the parents. In hindsight, maybe I should have suggested that she take someone to help her on the trip to the mall.

It was late Saturday afternoon when my cell phone rang. It was Track Star's mother. My heart skipped a beat. My first words were, "How is Track Star?" She hurriedly assured me that she was fine. But she went on to tell me that she had worn a tether on her arm and attached the other end to Track Star's arm as they moved around the mall.

According to her, everything was going surprisingly well, so she decided to release the tether from Track Star's arm. She was in one of the stores when an announcement was made over the intercom and the sound sent Track Star running before she had a chance to grab hold of her.

Before it was all over, Track Star knocked several displays down in the store, ran into the glass door where she cut her face, the mother sustained a sprained ankle and it took two security guards to catch and hold Track Star so she would not run into traffic. She said they both had to ride home in a cab since her ankle was too swollen to drive, and she had to ask her neighbor to take her sister back to the mall to pick up her car. She said, "Ms. Lena, never again will I ever take her anywhere."

One of the deficits with children who have autism is that they are often unable to tolerate high-pitched and loud sounds. Many are also sensitive to smell and texture.

My recommendation to parents is take the child on as many short trips as possible so as to help desensitize and teach the child how to manage in different situations.

I personally don't believe that because the child is sensitive to surroundings that the child should be kept in a bubble. This child is going to grow up and will have to learn to tolerate his environment and manage himself.

In school, Track Star was taken on community trips at least twice weekly. Her school was in walking distance of the library, museum and the park. We were usually on high alert when she was out. She tried on several occasions to run, but did not succeed. She slowly became tolerant of most of the environmental sounds and had stopped covering her ears most of the times.

It was a beautiful sight to behold when Track Star sat with the rest of the children and listened as the percussion band played in the park. She did not cover her ears. Not once did she attempt to run. I am very hopeful that over time, Track Star will continue to become more tolerant to unpleasant sounds and smells. Like I am sure her mother's hope is, my hope is that she will grow up to find her way without anyone having to chase her down. Hope is a mother's savior.

LITTLE Q

In all the years of working with children with special needs, there was never a potty challenge I did not welcome. Little Q was unlike any other. He was verbal. I might add, he was rather verbose. He talked consistently and at times incoherently. He was the most verbal in the class.

He would not however, use the words "pee pee" or "potty." He would stand there tattling about another child while he went in his pants. He was put on a half hour schedule where he had to sit for three minutes every half hour. He would sit on that potty and told everything about everyone, but he would not use the potty. He managed to pee and poop on himself every single day.

His parents seemed as baffled and frustrated at home as we were at school. We were always changing him. The boy was five and he was a big eater, too.

One day after eating corn, mashed potatoes, ground beef, and drinking milk, he went on himself while he was eating. The room had to be evacuated and sterilized. It was quite disheartening. He was a talker, yet he wouldn't say when he had to "go" and when he was taken, he didn't "go." When the parents arrived that evening, I told them we had to develop some other strategies. The parents suggested a plan in which he should not to be allowed to get up until he did what he was supposed to do.

I had to call the caseworker and the principal in on this matter. As the teacher, I wanted to support the parents, but I had to make sure I was in compliance. I was not prepared to violate any rules. How long was too long for Little Q to sit on the potty?

I needed something in writing or further clarification. Well, his schedule was modified from every half hour to every fifteen minutes. Yes! We lived in the bathroom. One more assistant had to be added.

The next morning as soon as he came in, his new schedule was put in place. He sat on the potty before breakfast and soon thereafter. I said to myself, "Today, you are going to poop in this potty." He was attempting to get up before the timer went off, but the assistant made him sit back down. He started to cry and acted as if he was struggling.

Sure enough he pooped in the toilet. The assistant named it "super poop." Little Q never had another accident on himself for the remainder of his stay in my class. The parents were elated. They, too, were tired of changing a five-year-old in diapers.

For the parents who are about to throw their hands up because they just can't seem to potty train their child, I'd say please do not give up. Be willing to try other strategies and work as a team. You will succeed if you keep pushing.

Talk to the child's teacher, case worker, and nurse, as well as other parents. It is better to find a way now than later. You do not want to have to be changing your child's Pampers when he is ten or older. The sooner you can have the child master this goal, the better everyone's life will be.

Never give up! You can give in and take a break, but get right back on track, and don't be afraid to seek help when you feel overwhelmed.

DANCER

The first day he came to visit and observe my class, he bounced in ahead of his parents and the case worker. The class was in the middle of Circle Time. By the time his parents entered the room, he was already in all of the play areas. He was drawn to the music corner. He started banging on the drums. That performance brought my Circle Time activities to an abrupt end. The other children crowded around while I introduced myself to the little dancer who was beating away at the drums.

I didn't get a verbal response, but he had the most beautiful smile and the whitest set of teeth. The parents nervously apologized for the sudden interruption by their son. I gave them a tour of the room. I told them I liked the energy that their son brought. They complained that he was too hyper, and it was hard for them to control him.

I felt that Dancer would be a good fit for my class, but of course the parents would have the final say as to the placement.

The parents agreed to the placement and Dancer became a member of my class. He caught on to the rhythm of the Circle Time songs very quickly. He danced throughout the circle activities each day. It seemed like he had music in his head, to which he was always bobbing. His attention span was fleeting, except when he was in the music corner, where he wanted to play every instrument another child picked up. Learning to share and take turns was one of my goals for him.

A turn-taking program was developed for him and he would be required several times a day to sit one-on-one with an aide to practice sharing and waiting for his favorite toy. He also had to learn to wait and share with another child.

Eventually he started to generalize this skill in a small group of three children. He started to use functional words and phrases. He learned to count to rhythmic beats and he soon made progress in other areas of language development. He became the "star" of my class performances with his smooth moves.

Dancer graduated from my class, but I was always kept abreast of his progress and he would say my name when we met in the gym, hallway or assemblies. Dancer went on to an inclusion school with in-class support for speech and other related services. Dancer is now in high school and I hope, with the continued support of his school and family, he will grow up to enjoy a manageable level of independence.

Our children do grow up. Whether or not they have a disability, all our hopes and dreams as parents and teachers have to be the same. We have to kindle the ember in every child's heart. We hope for all our children to grow into successful contributing members of the community. Children with autism do inspire. They are no different from other children. They just have a disability. As parents, our hopes and aspirations should be filled with the same level of intensity for all our children.

HI PITCH

I could not have chosen a more appropriate pseudonym than Hi Pitch. When he became frustrated, frightened or angry, our eardrums were in for a "workout." He had an aversion to textures. He would eat only crunchy foods like Cheerios, cornflakes, chicken nuggets, celery and other such foods. He was deathly afraid of soft textures such as play dough, shaving cream, Jell-O, glue and finger paint. One day he inadvertently picked up a Gummy Bear and he ran around the classroom screaming and flapping his hands as if he were being attacked.

One of his strengths was verbal expression. He was also being potty trained by his mom when he came to school. His receptive skills were also good.

Different materials were used to reinforce learning skills. He was slowly but constantly introduced to materials he liked as well as materials he did not like to touch. We had to negotiate with him to touch the "unpleasant" materials like glue and play dough. Working with all children involves negotiation. Children with autism are no different.

If we were working on an art project which required gluing, he would at least have to help to squeeze the glue out of the bottle and spread it with a brush so he could finish his work. He could then play with whatever his preferred toy was. With the play dough, he at first would only touch it with a roller or some other tool like a cookie cutter. One day he poked the dough with his fingers. Ah! Ah! He was realizing that the dough was not going to hurt him.

He slowly started to pinch and pull the dough and made it a little ball. I was elated at his accomplishment. I put his ball in a zip lock bag and sent it home. His mom reported that she could hardly get him to put down the ball and she woke up to find it smashed under his pillow.

Another one of the challenges with Hi Pitch was that he refused to drink except from a sippy cup. The team encouraged his mother to wean him from the sippy cup. In school we offered him his drink from a regular cup. He had no barriers preventing him using a regular cup. He would scream and holler, but we just had to wait him out. It would have been easier to hand him the sippy cup so he would be quiet. However, I believed this was absolutely inappropriate behavior for a six-year-old. The kids who could talk were calling him "baby." We had to lose the sippy cup.

Our biggest battles over the sippy cup were usually on Mondays or after a holiday break, even though his mother had promised that she was not giving him the sippy cup at all. One morning, I just happened to look out my window just in time to see his mother handing him a sippy cup in the back seat of the car. “Mom, you are busted.” She was called in on the matter.

The caseworker told her if she was not ready to reinforce what we were trying to teach in school, she need to let the rest of the team members know. It was not fair for us to put pressure on High Pitch in school to use a regular cup when he was not being encouraged at home to do the same. I felt guilty putting mom on the spot, but she needed to be reminded that she had the last word. She again promised that she was going to get rid of the several sippy cups that she had at home.

The rest of the team regrouped and continued to help wean Hi Pitch away from the sippy cup. The battle decreased until eventually he was one of the “big boys.” Hi Pitch was as proud as a peacock. He was drinking from a regular cup.

I still remember the look on his mother’s face when we gave her the hand-printed artwork he had created in class. We all celebrated. He was potty trained, he had started to finger-paint, and he was drinking from a cup just like a regular six-year-old. Interestingly, he was not screaming as much when he did not get his way. There was more time to educate him in other domains.

His mother reported that he was beginning to try other foods that were not crunchy. Every little step is a victory and a sign of hope.

The Last Word

Learn to Accept the Gift

When a child is diagnosed with a disability, as parents we cannot help but sometimes ask "why my child?" Instead, I hope that parents find the courage to say "why not my child? My child can and will achieve success according to his abilities."

I try to encourage parents to accept their child as he is and not what they would like him to be. Manage the challenges and see beyond the barrier of the disability. Every child is a precious gift and as parents we need to dig deep beyond the self-guilt and see the beauty and uniqueness of each child. From working with these children I have learned to be accepting of all children. I have also learned that one's echelon or strata in life does not protect or insulate one from having disappointments and unfulfilled dreams. No doubt, having a child with autism is a great challenge for many families and can be a leap into the unknown.

I once listened to a lecturer who described her experience of having a child with special needs as: *Planning for a dream vacation with your best friend to a country you always wanted to visit. After all the planning you arrive at your destination only to find out you have arrived in the wrong country, not understanding the language, not dressed for the climate, or right currency.*

One of my colleagues who was listening with me whispered, *and they do not accept credit cards.*

Nowadays, parents do not have to feel as if they are lost when dealing with a child with autism as more and more information is readily available to help parents cope. The Autism Society of America points out that even though there is "no single known cause or cure they stress the importance of research and of parents being involved in the care of their children. The organization points out that autism is treatable. Children do not "outgrow" autism, but studies show that early diagnosis and intervention can lead to significantly improved outcomes. With the right services and supports, people with autism can live full, healthy and meaningful lives."

My wish is that one day there will be a cure for Autism, but until then I wish the world can learn tolerance, patience and be inspired by these children. Because, for these children every little pebble of victory is a mountain of success. Hope is indeed a savior.

A Few Useful Tips for Parents

My child is always itching and trying to remove his shirt.

Try moisturizing skin and cut out all the labels. Dress him in cotton under shirts

My child does not speak. He points, screams and tantrums to express his needs and wants.

Take pictures of the items, people, activities that he generally wants/needs. Give him a choice of pictures when he starts pointing so he can learn to select the pictures of the items he wants.

My child can talk but will not ask for what he wants. He will point to, grab or just wait for things to be handed to him.

Give the child the words and try holding out on giving the item until he repeats the word/phrase/sentences that represents the item. Read to the child, sing to the child and have sessions where he has to practice repeating or echoing the words that you say to him.

My child refuses to sit on the potty. Therefore, I cannot begin to potty train him.

Try the child-size potty. Start by just having him sit for a minute per sitting. Play games while he is sitting. Increase the time by increments up to three minutes. Keep a timer so the chime will indicate to the child that the session has ended. Practice repeatedly. You can start by having him sit on the potty every thirty minutes. Make modifications as needed. When he does "go," make a big deal about it. Praise and reward the child.

My child does not play with anyone.

Practice turn-taking with him using a favorite toy. Start with your saying, "It is your turn," and give the child the toy. Let him play for thirty seconds to minute. Stretch out your hand for the toy and say, "My turn." At first he may not want to give, but practice by taking his hand and putting the toy in your hand. Make a big deal when he does give up the toy willingly. Eventually have him share and wait for the toy with another child.

My child makes little or no eye contact. Sometimes I don't think he hears me.

Call the child's name and ask him to look at you. You may sometimes have to touch his chin or direct his face in your direction to help foster eye contact. Also, give directions in small increments and wait for the child to process.

My child gets overwhelmed, and acts out when we go out in public. I am embarrassed to take him out.

Take your child out to as many places as possible. Teach him to manage his behaviors in his environment. Modify the length of time, and if possible, ask someone to accompany you when take out your child. All children act out when they are overwhelmed. Your child with autism is not so different. If people stare or act insensitive, you can use it as a teachable moment for some who might be willing to listen.

Autism As Defined by the Autism Society

Autism is a complex developmental disability that typically appears during the first three years of life and affects a person's ability to communicate and interact with others. Autism is defined by a certain set of behaviors and is a "spectrum disorder" that affects individuals differently and to varying degrees. There is no known single cause for autism, but increased awareness and funding can help families today.

In December 2009, the Centers for Disease Control and Prevention issued their ADDM autism prevalence report. The report concluded that the prevalence of autism had risen to 1 in every 110 births in the United States and almost 1 in 70 boys. The issuance of this report caused a media uproar, but the news was not a surprise to the Autism Society or to the 1.5 million Americans living with the effects of autism spectrum disorder. Nonetheless, the spotlight shown on autism as a result of the prevalence increase opens opportunities for the nation to consider how to serve these families facing a lifetime of supports for their children.

Currently, the Autism Society estimates that the lifetime cost of caring for a child with autism ranges from $3.5 million to $5 million, and that the United States is facing almost $90 billion annually in costs for autism. This figure includes research, insurance costs and non-covered expenses, Medicaid waivers for autism, educational spending, housing, transportation, and employment, in addition to related therapeutic services and caregiver costs.

Know the Signs: Early Identification Can Change Lives

Autism is treatable. Children do not "outgrow" autism, but studies show that early diagnosis and intervention lead to significantly improved outcomes.

Here are some signs to look for in the children in your life:

Lack of or delay in spoken language

Repetitive use of language and/or motor mannerisms (e.g., hand-flapping, twirling objects)

Little or no eye contact

Lack of interest in peer relationships

Lack of spontaneous or make-believe play

Persistent fixation on parts of objects

Other characteristics include:

No fear of danger

Over or under sensitivity

May prefer to be by him/herself

May use gestures to indicate wants and needs

May echo words or phrases

May have inappropriate attachments to objects

May spin self or objects

Prolonged repetitive play

May insist on things/routines always being the same

May exhibit inappropriate laughter

May display tantrums for no apparent reason

May avoid cuddling

May exhibit self injurious behavior when upset, i.e. biting self or banging heads

May exhibit an overall difficulty interacting with others.

Causes of Autism

The research indicates that the cause of autism is likely biological, but this may not be the only cause. Evidence has shown that one in three people diagnosed with autism have had around one to two epileptic seizures by the time they reach adulthood. Also, autism tends to run in families, pointing to the possibility of genetics as the cause.

Types of Autism

As defined by the Autism Society of America (ASA): "Autism is a complex developmental disability that typically appears in the first three years of life and is the result of a neurological disorder that affects the normal functioning of the brain, impacting development."

In the areas of social interaction and communication skills, both children and adults with autism typically show difficulties in verbal and non-verbal communication, social interactions, and leisure or play activities.

Autism is one of five disorders that falls under the umbrella of Pervasive Developmental Disorders PDD), a category of neurological disorders characterized by "severe and pervasive impairment in several areas of development."

Pervasive developmental disorder (PDD)

Also called Atypical Autism.

Children with this disorder have many of the characteristics of autism, but not all the criteria associated with autism.

Asperger's Disorder

Children with this disorder do not have the usual language barriers associated with autism and are generally very intelligent. However, they do tend to struggle with social interactions, and can fixate on a particular object or subject they take an interest in, and talk about it constantly.

Retts Disorder

Retts is rather similar to autism, but presents only in girls.

The children begin to develop on target, but then begin losing some communication abilities. The symptoms of Retts can begin to occur between ages one and four.

Austism Over Time

The symptoms of autism tend to lessen as one grows older. Children diagnosed with autism during childhood years may exhibit different problems once they reach their teen years, i.e., depression or other behavioral problems. Other children with autism may show very few symptoms when they reach their teen and adult years.

Autism Treatments

Currently there is no cure for autism. The disorder is treated by working to help improve the person's ability to communicate and cope with the symptoms and deal with the repetitive behaviors.

Some medications have been used to help alleviate some of the symptoms associated with autism. Other professional disciplines have been incorporated to manage autism. Therapies and medications are the most common ways of treating autism. Many children learn to communicate and better manage the symptoms. Children with autism can learn to function and communicate.

Every person with autism is unique, and like all individuals, has a unique personality and combination of characteristics.

Some individuals who are mildly affected may exhibit only slight delays in language and greater challenges in social interactions.

Persons with autism also process and respond to information in unique ways, such as crying, exhibiting aggression, and tantrums. Many people with autism have sensory issues, such as sensitivity to textures, light and sounds. Some children with autism do learn to make eye contact and can show affection.

REFERENCES

Useful Sites, Networks, and Resources for Parents of Autistic Children

Autism Society of America. Find out about research and programs, get tips, learn about living with autism, autism news, resources, and even sensory-friendly film showings. http://www.autism-society.org/

Autism Speaks.This organization is promoting public education as well as research for a cure. They include information on early signs as well as other information, autism in the news, sponsor walk events, and offer family support through social networks and outreach. http://www.autismspeaks.org/

Talk Autism. With a database of professionals, a place for those seeking help to reach out with their requests, and online presentations offering information on a variety of topics this group offers support for parents and caregivers. http://www.talkautism.org/

Organization for Autism Research. This group was organized by parents and grandparents with autistic children and focuses on educating parents, teachers, and caregivers about autism through applied science. http://www.researchautism.org/

Unlocking Autism. Working to speak for those with autism by getting information to the public as well as providing parents with information about legislation, biomedical research, and more, this group is a great resource to stay on top of what's going on behind the scenes. http://www.unlockingautism.org/site/c.kiKTL8PMLrF/b.4438891/k.BE3F/Home.htm

National Autism Association. Educating and empowering families while funding research for autism are the goals of this organization. Learn about research projects; find help for families, and more. http://www.nationalautismassociation.org/

Autism Research Institute. This organization is the home to the Defeat Autism Now! approach that believes autism can be cured through biomedical intervention that moves the focus of treatment away from psychotropic drugs as a primary means of treatment. This site offers tons of information on autism. http://www.autism.com/

The Arc of the United States. This national group offers information and support for families and adults living with intellectual and developmental disabilities with local chapters that can offer services such as advocates to attend ARD meetings at your child's school, case management services, and respite care. http://www.thearc.org/

Autism Network International. This organization is run by adults with autism with the goals of self-help and advocacy for those with autism. http://www.autreat.com/

Autism Support Network. Find a group, connect with other members, or read what others have to share about their experiences with autism and Asperger's. http://www.autismsupportnetwork.com/

WeAreAutism.org. This social network is for those living with ASDs and allows opportunities for social connection and sharing. http://www.weareautism.org/

Learn the Signs. Act Early. Get plenty of information about child development from the information here that is designed to help parents, educators, and caregivers recognize developmental disorders in children from birth to 5 years. http://www.cdc.gov/ncbddd/actearly/index.html

Your Child: Autism, Autistic Spectrum Disorders (ASD) and Pervasive Developmental Disorders (PDD). From the University of Michigan Health System, this resource provides basic information about the various types of autism spectrum disorders. http://www.med.umich.edu/yourchild/topics/autism.htm

CDC Autism Information Center. Find early warning signs, learn about screenings and diagnosis, learn about treatment and therapy options, and read research about the suspected relationship between vaccinations and autism. http://www.cdc.gov/ncbddd/autism/

Autism Research at the NICHD. Learn about the autism research going on at the National Institute of Child Health and Development. http://www.cdc.gov/ncbddd/autism/index.html

Autism and Communication. Learn about autism and communication with the information here from the National Institute on Deafness and Other Communication Disorders. http://www.nidcd.nih.gov

MedlinePlus: Autism. This resource offers links to many articles and publications offering information on everything from the basics about autism to diagnosis and treatment to coping to clinical trials. http://www.nlm.nih.gov/medlineplus/autism.html

Autism Treatment Center of America. This organization is the home of the Son-Rise program, which approaches treatment through embracing what the autistic behaviors communicate about children with ASDs and working to discover and incorporate what motivates them into the treatment plan. http://www.autismtreatmentcenter.org/

The Maia Chung Autism & Disabilities Foundation in Jamaica This Jamaican organization attempts to address the educational, health needs as well as health coverage, employment capabilities and skills training and sexual and reproductive health of the individuals affected by both autism and other types of disabilities. http://www.facebook.com/pages/The-Maia-Chung-Autism-and-Disabilities-Foundation/100339660027871

Acknowledgment

I am grateful to my fellow teachers, paraprofessionals, speech therapists, occupational therapists, physical therapist and all the other support staff who work tirelessly to support the children that I teach. Thanks to Ms. Naz, Ms. Jamilah Deans and Mrs. Philomena Kaba who cheered me on throughout this project.

"It takes a village to raise a child," so it takes all of your support to bring this work to fruition. Thanks to Amanda Lovell for allowing me to use the picture of her son Chad Amir on the cover of the book. Thanks to Dr. Terisita Rogers of Seton Hall University for writing the Foreword. Dr. Crespo thank you for the numerous times that you have said to me, "Ms. Lena you need to put that in a book."

Thanks to my parents, Horace and Ethel McCalla who are no longer here, but remain with me in spirit. Because of their values and teaching, I am who I am today; a determined, strong and hard worker who always believe I can get it done.

Thanks to my husband Yahya, my son Nelson, all my nieces and nephews for whom this is a testament to the possibilities of not giving up and not losing hope. Thanks to all my friends and family who have supported me unconditionally.

About The Author

Lena McCalla Njee teaches children with autism in the Irvington School District, New Jersey where she received the *2011-2012 Teacher of the Year Award.*

As a special education teacher, she is trained to work with children having multiple disabilities. However, she specializes in & loves working with children diagnosed with autism.

"My greatest joys are the successes of my students, the tears I see in the parents' eyes when they say, 'My child spoke my name for the first time in five years.' When I get a hug with those little arms filled with finger-paint, my heart is filled with joy."

She is a graduate of New Jersey City University where she earned a bachelor's degree in psychology and a master's degree in special education. Previously, she graduated from Sam Sharpe Teacher's College in Jamaica then migrated to the United States. Prior to her current position at the Irvington School District, she taught at Chad Elementary in Newark as well as Mount Carmel Guild School for Children with Disabilities.

McCalla Njee is a member of the Autism Society of America. She currently resides in New Jersey with her family.

www.ingramcontent.com/pod-product-compliance
Lightning Source LLC
LaVergne TN
LVHW100200061126
851857LV00010B/342
9780982963081